Fiddle
With a Riddle

Fiddle
With a Riddle
WRITE YOUR OWN RIDDLES

by Joanne E. Bernstein

illustrated by Giulio Maestro

E. P. DUTTON · NEW YORK

Many thanks to those whose riddle touches added up to a gaggle: the students and teachers of the Astor Program, Brooklyn, New York; Robin, Andrew, and Michael Bernstein; Paul Cohen; and, for the title, Bobbye Goldstein.

Library of Congress Cataloging in Publication Data

Bernstein, Joanne E.   Fiddle with a riddle.

SUMMARY: Outlines ways to write riddles using famous names, spelling tricks, metaphors, common expressions, and jokes.
1. Riddles—Authorship—Juvenile literature.
[1. Riddles—Authorship]   I. Maestro, Giulio.   II. Title.
PN6367.B4 808'.066'3986 79-11391 ISBN: 0-525-29678-6

Published in the United States by E. P. Dutton, a Division of Elsevier-Dutton Publishing Company, Inc., New York

Published simultaneously in Canada by Clarke, Irwin & Company Limited, Toronto and Vancouver

Editor: Ann Troy   Designer: Giulio Maestro

Printed in the U.S.A.
10 9 8 7 6 5 4 3 2

For Shirley

Contents

Introduction

All over the world, people laugh at puzzling questions and their surprising answers. But laughing is only part of the fun. Riddles also make you think. They help you to see something in a way you've never seen it before.

It's possible that you've already made up some riddles of your own. If you have, this book will help you to write more riddles. If you haven't begun making riddles, this book will get you started.

You're probably a rabid riddle-reader. Perhaps you've gone through every riddle book on your library's shelves. You may wonder if there are any riddles left to be made. The comedian Steve Allen says that we will never get to the last joke until we get to the last human being. Likewise, we will never get to the last riddle until we get to the last human being. Language is riddled with possibilities for good humor.

In preparing this book, I went through every riddle and joke book I could get my hands on. I studied the way riddles were constructed, looking at what made them clever. I also worked with groups of young people, helping them write their own riddles, and I wrote some of my own.

Sure enough, the young people and I developed riddles which were truly original: riddles which we didn't see printed anywhere. And the more we did it, the better we got at it. Some of the riddles we made up are in this book.

As you look through this book, you will see that many new riddles are not formed by thinking of questions and making up funny answers. Instead, they are created backwards. You find the answers first, and then look for appropriate questions which make the answers funny. Creating riddles backwards is not cheating. It just happens to be the easiest, most natural way to do it. It's the way most riddles are formed.

Usually, riddles present questions to be answered, but they don't have to be in that form. Some riddles consist of a simple sentence or two. The audience must guess what the tricky words are describing.

As long as I eat, I live.
But when I drink, I die.
> *Fire*

Many eyes,
never cries.
> *A potato*

As you start making riddles, some peculiar things may happen. One day you make a terrific riddle. The next day, you find it in a book! Or you may write a winner that you're very proud of. Bingo! A friend of yours writes a riddle that's almost the same.

Does this seem eerie? These things happen for several reasons, but there is no telepathy or ESP involved. More than one person can write the same riddle because people everywhere have similar concerns. They're likely to wonder about some of the same things.

It also happens because we all share the same meanings for words and might fiddle with those words until we work out the same jokes with them.

Finally, it happens because of the nature of humor. If *you* think it's funny, other young people may think so, too. Chances are, somewhere on this globe, someone

Many eyes,
never cries.
    A potato

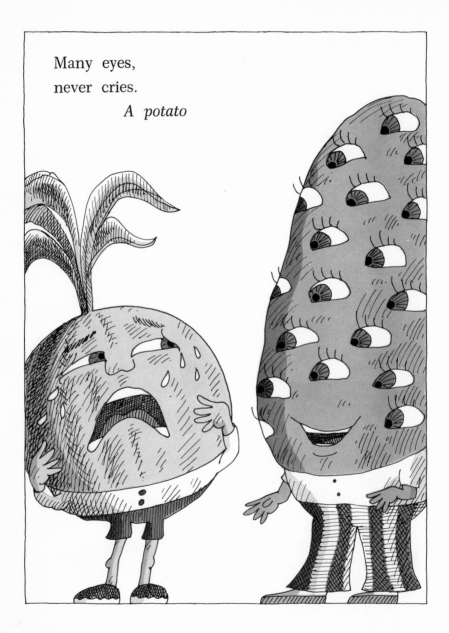

else has strung words together in a similar fashion. In fact, if you go back to the library shelves to study riddle and joke books from around the world, you'll see something surprising. People from countries as different as Iceland and Turkey may enjoy riddles that are almost identical. Sometimes only a word or two is changed from country to country.

It doesn't matter if a riddle remains yours, forever and ever. You could even say that if you find someone else writes a riddle like yours, it means you've *both* used words well.

One other thing. Please don't worry if people moan "O-a-u-g-h!" when you tell your own riddles. Joseph T. Shipley, a word game expert, says that the groans you hear are those of envy. It's a sign that others are just sorry *they* didn't think of it first. Every moan is really a compliment.

Happy riddling!

Turn a Joke
Into a Riddle

Easy riddles can be made by taking jokes you know and turning them into riddles.

You may like this joke—

"Tommy's tooth fell out," cried Bobby.

"Quick, get the toothpaste!" answered his mother.

To make it into a riddle, look at the punch line. The punch line is usually the last line, the words that get the laugh.

In this joke, the funny line is "Quick, get the tooth-paste!"

After you decide which words make up the punch line, think about all the words that came before it. Try to find a way to make those words into a question.

In the joke about Tommy's toothpaste, you might make this riddle question: "What do you do when your tooth falls out?"

The answer to this question is, of course, "Get the toothpaste."

But there is more than one way to put a question. You might like to keep that boy Tommy in your riddle. Then your question might be something like this: "What did Tommy do when his tooth fell out?" Now the answer would be, "He got the toothpaste."

Here's another joke which became a riddle in the hands of a creative young person. The joke went like this—

Did you hear the one about the jump rope?
Oh, skip it.

Now, turned into a riddle by someone who knew the ropes—

Knock, knock.
Who's there?
Jump rope.
Jump rope who?
Oh, skip it.

What do you do when
your tooth falls out?
Get the toothpaste.

You know plenty of jokes, so you don't need a list of jokes to get you started. Here's a sample—a joke about a joke, in fact—to kick off with.

Laura heard a good joke and was going to take it home, but she decided against it. That was carrying a joke too far.

Where's the punch line? How can you change the joke into a riddle? Is there some way you can add your own touch? What will you change?
Now try this joke.

He gave a moving performance. Everyone moved to the nearest exit.

Riddle Parallels

If you can never get enough riddle books, you've probably noticed that many riddles are very similar. Authors juggle old favorites around. They fiddle here and fiddle there and—lo and behold—a brand-new, satisfying riddle appears!

You can do this, too.

Let's begin with the familiar riddle, "How many rocks can you put into an empty hole?" The answer is "None, then the hole wouldn't be empty."

The hole riddle pattern can be reworked endlessly, and it still comes out whole. Here are some parallel variations made up by two girls in New York.

How many pencils can you put into an empty bookbag?

How many candies can you put into an empty jar?

Both these riddles have the traditional answer, "None, then it wouldn't be empty." But you needn't stick to the traditional response in order to have a complete riddle. Two fellows came up with this—

How many carrots can you feed a hungry rat?
None, rats don't like carrots.

Many new riddles can be made from this riddle pattern—"What goes zzub, zzub?" The answer is "A bee flying backwards," but here are some original variations.

What goes muy, muy?
> *Someone eating ice cream backwards*

What goes chit-chat, tick-tock, boom-bang?
> *A sick clock*

What goes ʇǝǝʍʇ-ʇǝǝʍʇ?
> *A bird sitting on her eggs upside down*

What goes away, away, and up?
> *Stupidman*

How would your "What goes . . . ?" riddle go?

Now try the riddle, "What's black and white and red all over?" For years, the answers have been "a newspaper" or "an embarrassed zebra."

Here's a new response that will *really* make you

What goes ʇǝǝʍʇ-ʇǝǝʍʇ?
   A bird sitting on her eggs
   upside down

groan! For one girl, the obvious answer was a chocolate sundae with ketchup on top! Do you suppose this will start a trend?

LOGIC AT PLAY

Some riddles are funny just because the answers are the logical truth. In these riddles, often there is no joke at all, only the unexpected voice of reason. You've probably heard many such riddles.

Some old standards—

How many months have 28 days?
> *All of them*

Why don't you put an ad in the paper when your dog is lost?
> *Dogs can't read.*

What is a kitten after it is four days old?
> *Five days old*

How long is a piece of string?
> *Twice the distance from the middle to the end*

By changing just one or two words, you can have a new riddle. In the last riddle, *a piece of string* can become *a pencil*. In the kitten riddle, *kitten* can become a *baby giraffe*. And so on.

You can take almost any subject and make a logic riddle from it. You might try out some of these subjects:

shoelaces	music
school bus	whispering
television	laughing
blankets	desk
hamburger	mice

Here are two kids' logic riddles made from the last subject on the list—

Why do cats eat mice?
> *Because they're hungry.*

What did the mouse say when he ate up the words?
> *I don't know. He ate the words to this joke.*

You've probably heard this riddle—

What has four wheels and flies?
> *A garbage truck*

What did the mouse say
when he ate up the words?
I don't know. He ate
the words to this joke.

One girl's parallel was—

> What has three wheels and flies?
> *An airplane*

How else can logic riddles go? Let's look at others young people made up. First, a long one.

> A boy got the gift he wanted most in the world.
> He had waited months and months to get
> it. When he finally got it, what do you think
> he said?
> *Thank you.*

Now, two short ones.

> What happens if you cross a book
> and a lunch box?
> *Nothing.*
> Why does the world go round and round?
> *It can't jump up and down.*

KNOCK-KNOCKS

Riddle parallels don't always have to be logical. They can be silly as anything. Knock-knock jokes are really silly riddles. They've been popular for decades.

People continue to enjoy them, and new books of knock-knocks continue to be published.

There seems to be no end to knock-knock parallels, because there's no limit to the way real names and silly names can be put together.

One boy made up this joke about his own name.

Knock, knock.
Who's there?
Andy.
Andy who?
     Andybody home?

There are many other real names you can play with. Riddle power is easily found in such names as Wanda, Juan, Howard, and Ida. Also, Ceil, Ken, and Sally. Can you do anything with your own?

But you don't need real names to play knock-knock. Here are some riddles written by nine-year-olds—

Knock, knock.
Who's there?
Tuba.
Tuba who?
     Tuba toothpaste

Knock, knock.

Who's there?

Orange juice.

Orange juice who?

     Orange juice sorry you asked?

Knock, knock.

Who's there?

Abacus.

Abacus who?

     Abacus on the cheek? (Have a kiss?)

Thank you, I will.

Spelling Trick Riddles

For many young people, spelling is a struggle—a necessary but boring exercise for the memory, involving pretests, retests, and endless writing. Actually, spelling and spelling tricks can provide hours of exciting riddle fun.

Here are some of the ways.

I C U

The I-C-U riddle is probably the easiest kind of riddle to construct. To make an I-C-U, all you have to do is think about the letters of the alphabet and the ways they are identical or similar to actual words.

The three letters I, C, and U make a short sentence. To make a riddle out of them, just ask a question for which the answer is I C U.

My question is, "What letters of the alphabet come after peek-a-boo?" I C U fits the bill. Perhaps you have another question which also fits.

You may have seen these sample I-C-U riddles in books.

What letter separates Europe from America?
>C

What letter is a female sheep?
>U

What letters are a tent?
>T-P

What letters are the smartest?
>Y's

You can use numbers, too, as in this one—

Which number is important in racing?
>1

To get started on your own, take a look at these, which other young people wrote. Some of them played with the letters, changing the sounds in funny ways.

What does my mother call me?
>A U

Which letter is the
most important person?
I

Which letter is the most important person?

I

What one letter is reading my jokes?

U

What do little army people drive?

G-P's

What letters smell?

P-U

What letters are a vegetable?

B-N

You can even use letters and numbers together. Here are three riddles which combine letters and numbers—

What is a dog?

K-9

Who is from another country?

4-N-R

Who is a singer?

10-R

And here are some good riddling letters and numbers 4 U 2 C: A, B, J, P, U, L, I, T, 8, 2, 4, 1, etc.

What letters smell?

P-U

SPELL CLOUD IN FOUR LETTERS.

Can you spell *cloud* in four letters? It usually has five, but you can test both spelling and cleverness at the same time when you ask tricky questions.

When someone asks you how to spell *frozen water* in three letters, at first it seems impossible. But then, aha—*ice* has three letters! And ice is frozen water.

Spelling tricks of this type are very easy to make up. Take a look at these original ones by boys and girls.

Spell *chicken, turkey,* and *hot dog* in four letters.
    M-E-A-T

What three letters are crooks afraid of?
    F-B-I

How do you spell *broken glass* in four letters?
    O-U-C-H

What country spells *fragile* in five letters?
    C-H-I-N-A

By the way, the answer to the title riddle above is R-A-I-N.

CHANGE-A-LETTER

Change-a-letter riddles are made when you alter one letter (or more) in a word to create a new idea.

You've probably seen these. Many of them focus upon the letter S, for it's a versatile letter. It can be both dangerous and scary.

When is it dangerous? When it changes *laughter* into *slaughter*.

And how is it scary? When it changes *cream* into *scream*.

Then there is the letter D, never a popular letter on spelling tests. In fact, the letter D on a spelling test makes *Ma mad*.

Have you seen these change-a-letter riddles?

What is the difference between *here* and *there*?
>   *The letter T*

Make morning feel sorry for itself.
>   *Add a U to make it mourning.*

Can you make any like that? Youngsters came up with these—

How do you spell a pig blindfolded?
>   *P-G without an I* (eye)

How do you make bears listen?
>   *Take away the B and they're all ears.*

In making your own change-a-letter riddles, remem-

Make morning feel sorry for itself.

Add a U to make it mourning.

ber that you can add a letter anywhere in the word. Or you can take away any letter.

ANAGRAMS

A cousin of change-a-letter is the game of anagrams. In this spelling trick, you don't add letters or take them away, you simply rearrange them.

To make anagrams, think of some of the short words you know. It's best to start off with three-letter words. When you've done it a few times, it's easier to move on to longer words.

Write some three-letter words down. Can any of them be turned into new words if you read them backwards? Might they become new words if you throw the letters in the air and watch them land in mixed-up ways? If they can, then you have juggled your way into some anagrams.

Now they have to be made into riddles.

Let's take the word *pan*. It turns into another word when read backwards. The word, of course, is *nap*. To create a full anagram riddle, you must find a definition or description for the word *nap*.

This is how the *pan-nap* anagram might look—

Change PAN into a short sleep.

NAP

Some three-letter anagrams by kids—

Change DAM into an angry mood.

MAD

Change EAT into something to drink.

TEA

Change WON into the opposite of then.

NOW

And here are some original four-letter anagrams—

Change LOOP into a place to swim.

POOL

Change MOAT into the smallest component of an element.

ATOM

Change NAME into a synonym for cruel.

MEAN

Change MEAT into people who race together.

TEAM

Change MEAT into
people who race together.
TEAM

Did you notice any other anagrams that can be made from the letters in the last two samples?

Once you begin to notice that more than one anagram is possible, you can work your way up. For example, how many spelling combinations do you think there are in the word *post*? If you don't stop at two or three, you're tops!

Double Meaning Riddles

Very likely the first funny things you said came about when you noticed that a word had two meanings. Putting the two very different meanings together in a sentence made a joke.

Double meanings are sometimes called plays on words, or puns. Riddles which use plays on words are sometimes called conundrums.

Once you become alert to double meanings you can make more riddles. You can make better riddles. In fact, you can drive everyone crazy, seeing two meanings when others see just one. But always remember, people who groan really admire you.

How can you notice double meanings more? There's only one way, and that is to practice. On everything. One idea is to say or write down the words which come into your mind just as quickly as you can. Go from the first word, to the next, and to the next, writing down as many as you can as fast as you can. Then look back on your list for double meanings. The process of saying or writing everything which comes into your head is called free association. One idea soon leads to another.

Another way to practice is to get together with friends and brainstorm. You brainstorm when you talk freely and put your ideas together. Free association in a group will help you all to get your ideas into focus. (As a wise person once said, "Many clouded minds can amount to great brainstorms." That person also warned that pooling ideas might lead to nothing more than water on the brain. But every effort aimed at helping riddles pour forth is worthwhile.)

If you decide to brainstorm, take a category and build as many puns in that area as you can, shooting the double meanings out in a rapid stream. Try it in a group. You'll see that you all get better and better.

A glimpse into the animal world should start you off at a gallop. Play with the animals' names, the way they look, the things they do.

To help you have a whale of a time, here are some of the animal pun riddles other kids made up.

What did the buck call his doe?

Deer (of course)

What did the male bee call his queen?

Honey (another easy one)

Why did Danny tell his mother there was an
animal in the tub with him?

Because he was bare

When is a dog overweight?

When it's a husky

What do you call a pet who chews on furniture?

Gnaw-ty

In what room can a lion watch TV?

The den

What do you get when you cross an insect with
a horse and wagon?

A buggy

How did the stegosaurus eat his meals?

On his plates

What's on your head and runs?

A hare

How does an ape fix a leaky faucet?

With a monkey wrench

Which animal will give you dessert off his back?

A chocolate moose

What do you call a pet
who chews on furniture?
    Gnaw-ty

Food is another category which you may relish. Try "pudding" your brains together as these kids did. Taste their treats:

Which vegetable has asthma?
> *An artichoke*

Why does someone who fries potatoes get very little sleep?
> *He starts out oily.*

What do you call someone who bakes like crazy?
> *A dough-nut*

What kind of lollipop is a fool?
> *A sucker*

Why did the man have a pain in his side at dinner?
> *He ate his liver.*

What food do the best skaters prefer?
> *Ice cream*

Why can't you eat a sunflower seed?
> *It's too hot.*

What do vampires have for dinner?
> *Human beans*

How do you make a cucumber laugh?
> *Pickle it.* (Tickle it.)

What do vampires have
for dinner?

Human beans

What did the hungry twins say in the womb?

Fetus, fetus. (Feed us, feed us.)

What did one angry pretzel say to another?

I've never been so insalted!

Notice, sometimes you change the word around a bit to get a riddle. Some of these, like the pretzel riddle, have a little twist to them.

Try to find more animal and food riddles. Some other good categories for double meanings and brainstorms include trees, plants, flowers, money, clothing, and furniture.

Once you get started punning, it's hard to stop. Here is an assorted bunch of double meaning riddles concocted by young riddle makers.

What color should you paint a garbage can?

Pail green

What kind of fence is always arguing with the mayor?

Picket

Who made the tides?

The sea sons, who blew on the ocean

What kind of tree makes music?

A sapsophone

What is a book about the history of cars called?

An auto-biography

What famous person can publish a newspaper?

A press-ident

What did one candle say to the other?

Let's make trouble. We're both wick-ed.

What did the pillow say to the quilt?

Comfort-er me, I'm feeling down.

Read these next two, one right after another, fast:

What do you call an infant who holds his breath?

Little Boy Blue

How did the little boy clear his stuffed nose?

Little boy blew

Expression Riddles

Many riddles can be made from everyday expressions. Riddle makers think about the words in an expression. They look at the two meanings, the figurative and the literal. You've heard people say that "a little goes a long way." This expression is a figurative way to say stretch out what you have and be thrifty. Riddle makers know this, but they also look at the literal meaning—the exact meaning of each and every word.

Soon a relationship between the figurative and literal meanings appears. A riddle is likely to result.

Why do giraffes have such small appetites?
Because a little goes a long way

To find expressions to work with for your own riddles, think of categories, such as colors. List all the expressions you know which mention a color. Look at their figurative meanings, then look at their literal meanings. Is something funny hiding there? If so, you've found a pun, or a double meaning, and you have the workings of a good riddle.

Here's a short list of expressions to get you in the pink.

red in the face	bluenose
feeling blue	yellowbelly
white as a sheet	in the black

And here's a riddle created from a colorful expression—

Why was the clock embarrassed every time someone looked at him?
   Because he was read in the face

Now let's elbow up to parts of the body and give them the eye.

two left feet	right-hand man
pain in the neck	all thumbs
Achilles' heel	nosy
tennis elbow	clearheaded
soft shoulder	nose to the grindstone
finger in every pie	ear to the ground

It's not as hard as it looks. These riddles were made by a young girl who used her head. You might say she "nose all the ankles."

Why did the snake lose the argument?
> *He didn't have a leg to stand on.*

Why are some people afraid of winter?
> *They have cold feet.*

And here are more riddles created from other expressions boys and girls knew.

Why is it embarrassing to sit in a theatre?
> *The actors are always creating a scene.*

How are the turkey and the guests alike on Thanksgiving?
> *Both get stuffed.*

What did the mouse say when the cat bit its tail?
> *That's the end of me!*

Why is a trampoline dangerous?
> *You might jump to a conclusion!*

Where is the planet Pluto?
> *Out of this world.*

What happens if you eat poison ivy?
> *You start making rash promises.*

Why did the snake
lose the argument?
*He didn't have a leg
to stand on.*

Why do you have to cook vegetables very carefully?
Otherwise you might spill the beans.

How do you like these kids' riddles? The boys and girls took expressions and twisted them around to sound funny.

What does the dentist say when you enter
the office?
Gum on in.
What did one knitting needle say to the other?
Where there's a wool, there's a way.

At the beginning, it may be hard to think of expressions. Go to newspapers and magazines for inspiration.

Two kids recently thumbed through a magazine. An ad for the Yellow Pages announced, "We tell you where to go." That expression begged to become a riddle, so one girl came up with this—

When do crossing guards make people mad?
When they tell them where to go

Another page showed an ad with the expression "You send me." Not to be outdone, another girl riddled—

What did the letter say to the letter carrier?
You send me.

What did the letter
say to the letter carrier?
　　　You send me.

You might want to work on riddles with a group of people. Some expressions lead to several riddles, each of them good. Together you and your partners can knead the material, much as you would knead dough, until you are satisfied with what you've done. Needless to say, there are riddles in the phrase "knead dough." Can you find them?

"HOW'S BUSINESS?"

One kind of riddle that uses expressions is called "How's business?"

The form is simple: You announce you're in a particular business—say, the laundry business.

Your friend then responds: "How's business?"

At this point, it's up to you to supply the funny saying.

For the laundry business, you might say "I'm cleaning up" or "I'm pressing my luck," but there are many other good answers.

The responses have to say something about the way a business is going—is it succeeding or failing? Is it hard or easy? Are the customers satisfied? At the same time, the response has to be related to some aspect of the business you are discussing. In a laundry, you clean and press.

"How's business?" has been a popular parlor game because these riddles are so easy to make. They can be enjoyed by people of all ages.

As is the case with so many other types of riddles, "How's business?" riddles come to mind easily if you try working in category groupings. Here are some samples, using variations of the "How's business?" form in order to make it more interesting.

Sports

Marcia is in the deep-sea diving business.
How's business?
She's in over her head.
I'm a basketball player.
What do you think of it?
It makes me throw up!

Restaurants

I run an Italian restaurant.
How's it going?
I'm finally getting a pizza the pie.

On the other hand, Julia enjoys the Chinese restaurant business. Do you know why? She's making a fortune, cookie. (Chinese cooking is also easy. All it takes is a little wok.)

Doctors (a rich source of laughs)

Did you hear about the surgeon who couldn't make much money?

He ran a cut-rate operation.

That didn't compare with Dr. Sole, the podiatrist. When he was asked how his business was, he replied, "Terrible. All de-time I face de-feat."

And, of course, a good mugging is to be found in the . . .

Crime business

I'm in the pickpocket business.

How's business?

Touch and go.

Your turn now. How do you think business is for the robber?

While some "How's business?" riddles come to mind from thinking of categories, others just plain come. Like this one, created by a disgusted older brother—

I'm in the pickpocket business.
How's business?
Touch and go.

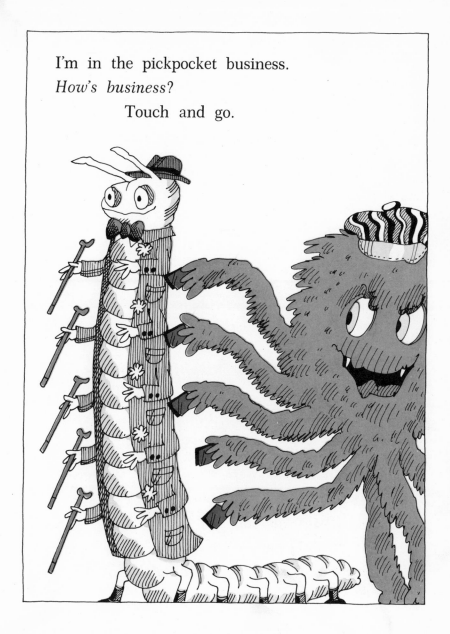

I'm in the diaper business.
How's business?
It stinks!
(There are some other good responses for
this changing business—have you any?)

Some "How's business?" riddles are short and sweet
like this—

Wanda makes wine.
How's business?
Grape!

Other "How's business?" riddles are silly . . . like
this—

I'm in the bird-beak collection business.
How's business?
Bills are piling up.

Many "How's business?" riddles lend themselves to
numerous suitable answers. You might make a list of
businesses and write some answers you like. Then compare laughs with your friends.

Here are some businesses to start with, along with
sample answers from the boys and girls I worked with.
See if you can top them.

- The barber business   (Cutting down)
- A beauty parlor   (It's permanent work.)
- Bowling   (Right up my alley)
- Electrician   (Delightful)
- Bakery   (There's no loafing.)
- Tailor   (Sew-sew)
- Diamond   (Hard)
- Finally, there's the zoo business, promising a menagerie of answers. That business has been called everything from wild to unbearable.

Famous Name Riddles

PLACE NAMES

You've probably heard some of the old jokes with place names in them.

Are you HUNGARY?
>Yes, SIAM.

What can we SERBIA?
>TURKEY and coffee with a CUBA sugar.

Another riddle, this time in poetry, is this—

Upon a hill there is a mill,
Around the mill there is a walk,
Under the walk there is a key.
What is the name of this city?
>MILWAUKEE

Twisting the names of places around to land new riddles is not hard to do. One bright girl played with the word Minnesota, saying it over and over again. Suddenly she realized it was the state in which some nasty people live. Why? It's *Mean*-isota!

Doing these will help sharpen your wits. And speaking of sharp, which state is sharp? Arkan*saw*, of course.

Oklahoma is another fine riddling state. One boy looked inside and found a hidden word, leading him to riddle—

In which state can you relax and be comfortable?
Okla-HOME-a

Here are more place-name riddles made up by young people:

Where do you find many horses?
In FILLY-delphia
What city can you eat?
The Big Apple
Where does Lassie live?
COLLIE-fornia

Play with some of these place names. See how many

What city can you eat?
The Big Apple

riddles you can make by rolling the names around on your tongue.

Buffalo	Catskills
Fiji	Greece
Iowa	New Jersey
Newark	China
Samoa	Tennessee
Texas	Thailand
Wales	

Sometimes it's the abbreviation of a place name that leads to a riddle. For example, did you know which city is the absolute worst? It's in Pennsylvania, and it's the Pitts.

Here are some other abbreviations which work well in riddles.

Ala.	Ark.
Mass.	Md.
Me.	Miss.
Mo.	Ore.
Pa.	Tenn.
Wash.	

Have you any more?

FAMOUS PEOPLE

What names do you suppose appear most frequently in the daily newspaper? Are they the names of government leaders? The names of presidents are candidates for good riddles.

One group of ten-year-olds brainstormed about the United States presidents. Here are the hardest riddles they made up. Which names answer these riddles?

Which president manufactured the Model T?
Which president's name is like a present?
Which president was always saying no?
Which president was a successful dentist?
Which president's name can cure you of illness?
> *Answers: Ford, Grant, Nixon, Fillmore,*
> *and Madison* (medicine)

Other presidents' names which work in riddles include Johnson, Truman, Washington, and Jackson. Also Pierce, Tyler, Taylor, Hayes, and Polk. And if you get very good at this, you can even try Lincoln two presidents' names together in one riddle!

Don't stop at the presidents' names. Think of the other famous people whose names you know. When the boys and girls I worked with ran out of names to try, they studied magazines and newspapers for new ideas. These are some of their riddles—

Do you know which pirate always wore metal underwear?

Long John Silver

Why do people read Tolkien?

It's hobbit-forming.

Why shouldn't you hit a famous composer?

Because he'll hit you Bach

Which famous American is sculpted most often?

George Washington Carver

Which famous patriot was a vegetable?

Uncle Yam

NAMES OF PRODUCTS

Making riddles out of names of objects and brands is not easy, but it *can* be done. Have you seen these in riddle books?

Why did Santa have only seven reindeer Christmas Eve?

Comet was home cleaning the sink.

What did the razor blade say to the razor?

Schick 'em up.

Which famous patriot
was a vegetable?
   Uncle Yam

One boy wrote these riddles:

Why did the girls cry when Tim kissed them?
He needed Kissterine.
What airplane does a violinist prefer?
Boeing (That riddle is viol.)

A Chinese girl wrote these two—

What does a Chinese limerick writer ride in?
A limerickshaw
What do you call an American barber?
A Yankee Clipper

Where are the products you could start riddling with? Everywhere. To spark you, why not begin with the names of today's cars?

Cars used to have plain names—Chevrolet, Ford, Volkswagen. Not anymore. The manufacturers give autos sporty, exciting concepts in the names, many of these new names coming from the animal world. The designers hope you will want to get in and roar away.

A sample—

Which car is a spotted horse?
A Pinto

How many riddles can you make from this list?

Rabbit	Impala
Fox	Beetle
Mustang	Road Runner
Wild Cat	Cobra
Colt	Maverick
Falcon	Firebird
Cougar	Sting Ray

Metaphor Riddles

A metaphor is a way to describe something by comparing it to something else. You might describe a stubborn person as a rock, or a weak person as a bowl of jelly. This word picture makes the audience imagine the real object or scene.

The audience must guess what's described. You can write your metaphor as a question, or it can be a few sentences or even a short phrase. Many riddle makers enjoy stumping friends with poetry.

Nature and the world around us are excellent sources for metaphors. This has been noticed all around the world. In the animal kingdom—

Taller sitting than standing
> *A dog* (This short tale comes from Borneo.)

Who eats at the king's table and doesn't
use a napkin?

> *A fly* (from West Africa)

And within the solar system—

Sometimes it is a plate,
Sometimes it is a long, thin boat.
Is it a plate or a boat?

> *The moon* (as seen in Burma)

Two horses, white and black,
chase each other forever in vain

> *Day and night* (Iran)

Here's an everyday object described four different
ways.

- What was made years ago, and is still being made
  today?
- Dressed, it does not go out.
- One head, one foot,
  One body, four legs
- It has four legs and a foot
  And can't walk.
  It has a head
  And can't talk.

Who eats at the king's table
and doesn't use a napkin?
  A fly

When did you know it was a *bed*?

Here is another set of metaphor riddles. This time they poetically depict something to eat. Try to crack the code.

- In a bowl of china are fixed
  Two liquids with colors unmixed.
- What is more useful when it is broken?
- White as the clouds,
  Yellow as the sun,
  If I fall I break.
  What am I?

These metaphors are about an *egg*.

It's hard to egg-zaggerate the number of eggs-quisite egg metaphors which exist. The most famous egg-zample is Humpty-Dumpty.

The subjects fit for metaphor riddles are many. Among them:

musical instruments	holidays
letters of the alphabet	colors
wind	table
television	water
animals	appliances

clouds	seasons
flowers	the year
trees	rings
clock	footprints
occupations	birds

Make your own. Perhaps some other metaphor riddles will stimulate you. These were done by young people who ranged between the ages of five and thirteen.

The mirror of winter

Ice

Gentle or rough as a beast,
I come from north, south, west, east.
What am I?

The wind

I make several points, but I can't talk.

A triangle

It takes your secrets,
But never keeps them.
It may capture you,
But you won't get hurt.

Snap! *A camera*

The mirror of winter
Ice

Swoosh, swoosh,
Diagonally down.
The swiftest, shiniest
Ride in town.
  A playground slide

It has teeth but doesn't chew.
  A key

Swallowing nearly everything that touches my lips,
I never really eat.
I'll never be happy.
I'm usually blue.
  A mailbox

It's long and short, cold and hot.
It goes around and around and never stops.
  The year

With eight even sides I wait and wait for cars to
come.
When they meet me they must do as I say and be
on time, for it is dangerous to be late.
I make them see red!
  A stop sign

I pass so quickly, but I'm always with you.
Time

Hands and a face,
Without a heart.
A clock

Here are three different metaphors done by kids, all about the same thing.

- Who is here, who is there, but nowhere?
- It copies you, only it is bigger or smaller than you.
- In an argument, whom can you always count on?

How many clues did you need to know that it was your *shadow*?

Riddle
Treasure Hunt

This is actually a game, developed one day by two young girls.

To make a riddle treasure hunt, you gather a bunch of riddles. The riddles can be original—or you can look for them in riddle or joke books.

Look for riddles which have answers that relate to things in your house or yard. Choose about four or five riddles.

Write each riddle, without the answer, on a small piece of paper. An index card, 3 inches by 5 inches, would be fine, too.

Number the papers or cards. These written questions are your clues.

Read clue number 1. Answer the riddle to yourself. Your answer will tell you the best place to hide clue number 2. Here's an example. Clue number 1 might be: What kind of fish is good on toast? You know that the answer is jelly. You place clue number 2 on top of the jelly jar in the refrigerator, just waiting to be found.

Think through all the clues and hide them where they belong. Your last clue will lead to the hunter's final destination. There will be no riddle there. At that location, the treasure hunt is over. Leave a small prize for the treasure hunter to find.

Now you're set.

Call your treasure hunter—a friend, parent, brother or sister. The game is about to begin. Give your hunter clue number 1, and see how long it takes to find the treasure.

This is the treasure hunt my friends sent me on. To start, I was given clue number 1—

• What business is best when things are dullest?

My next clue was found at the *knife sharpener*. It read—

• What never asks questions but demands answers?

That was hard, but eventually I found clue number 3 tucked under the *doorbell*.

• What do you do when the bathroom gets flooded?

What was the matter with
the house that was sick?
It had a pane.

Hard again. I was ready to throw in the towel, when I realized that expression was the answer!

Clue number 4 was in the *linen closet*—

• What musical instrument do you eat for dessert?

I fiddled with that for a while, then came up with *cello*. Sure enough, taped to the jello, was clue number 5—

• What was the matter with the house that was sick?

In a house with a lot of windows, it was hard to figure out which one had the *pane*, but it could be done. At the right window, I found the final clue, number 6—

• What has an eye but cannot see?

I went back to the refrigerator and inspected the potatoes—no clue, no treasure.

Think, think. At last! Yes, a *needle* also has an eye but cannot see. Way up at the top of the closet, in the sewing kit, I found my treasure—a shiny new dime!

Happy hunting! Enjoy the riddle business, and may all your troubles be riddle ones.